SCHOLASTIC

50+ Super-Fun Math Activities

1

by Cecilia Dinio-Durkin

NEW YORK • TORONTO • LONDON • AUCKLAND • SYDNEY
MEXICO CITY • NEW DELHI • HONG KONG • BUENOS AIRES

Teaching *Resources*

W9-ART-550

Edited by Jean Liccione

Cover design by Ka-Yeon Kim-Li

Interior design by Ellen Matlach Hassell for Boultinghouse & Boultinghouse, Inc.

Interior illustrations by Maxie Chambliss and Manuel Rivera

ISBN-13: 978-0-545-20810-9

ISBN-10: 0-545-20810-6

Printed in the U.S.A.

1 2 3 4 5 6 7 8 9 10   40   17 16 15 14 13 12 11 10

Contents

(continued on the next page)

✳ This activity includes a reproducible.

GEOMETRY AND SPATIAL SENSE

TIME

MONEY

MEASUREMENT

ASSESSING CHILDRENS' MATH LEARNING

✳ This activity includes a reproducible.

Introduction

Welcome to *50+ Super-Fun Math Activities: Grade 1*. This book contains a unique collection of activities that reinforce important first-grade-level mathematics concepts and skills and support the math standards recommended by the National Council of Teachers of Mathematics (NCTM). See page 6, for more.

The book is organized by nine major content topics. When you're teaching a particular math concept or skill, just check the Contents page. Browse the activities listed under each topic to find just the right one to reinforce students' learning. Each major topic has projects, games, activities, and ready-to-use reproducibles designed to reinforce specific learning objectives. The activities will also get students interested and excited, and encourage them to value math and become confident mathematicians.

ACTIVITY FEATURES

The activities include grouping suggestions, lists of needed materials, teaching tips, step-by-step directions, and easy Assessment ideas. Some activities also include the following features:

◆ Extensions and Variations—ideas for taking the math skills and concepts further

◆ Home Links—quick and easy activities students can do at home with their families

◆ Writing Connections—suggestions for encouraging students to communicate and reinforce what they've learned through writing.

ABOUT GROUPING

Sometimes it's important for students to work together in groups or pairs, to collaborate and communicate. Sometimes they need to work independently. The activities in this book support a variety of needs, from independent to whole class work. You'll find a grouping suggestion at the beginning of each activity.

ASSESSING STUDENTS' WORK

NCTM recommends a variety of approaches to assessment of the various dimensions of a student's mathematical learning. The following assessment suggestions are incorporated throughout this book:

◆ ideas for group and class discussion

◆ ideas for journal writing and written response

◆ ideas for ongoing informal teacher observations

On pages 61–63, you'll also find suggested ways of observing and keeping records of students' work as well as a reproducible student Self-Evaluation Form and an Assessment Checklist and Scoring Rubric.

Remember that you can review students' self-assessments and their journals and written responses to see not only how well they understand concepts but also how well they express their mathematical understandings.

CONNECTIONS TO THE MATH STANDARDS

The activities in this book are designed to support you in meeting the following process standards for students in grades PreK–2 recommended by the National Council of Teachers of Mathematics (NCTM):

Problem Solving The activities promote a problem-solving approach to learning. Throughout the book, you'll find suggestions for encouraging students to develop, apply, and explain their problem-solving strategies.

Reasoning & Proof Suggestions in the last step of each activity can serve as prompts to help students draw logical conclusions, explain and justify their thinking, and "pull it together" to make sense of the mathematics skills and concepts they've just used. Activities encourage students to use patterns and relationships as they work.

Communication Activities include ideas for helping students organize and consolidate their mathematical thinking through class discussions and writing connections.

Connections Activities tie to the real world, to the interests of first-grade students, and to other areas of the curriculum. The purpose of many activities is to bridge conceptual and procedural knowledge, and to bridge different topics in mathematics.

Representation Students use manipulatives, pictures and diagrams, and numerical representations to complete the activities.

The grids below show how the activities correlate to the other math standards for grades PreK–2.

PAGE	Number & Operations	Algebra	Geometry	Measurement	Data Analysis & Probability
9		◆			◆
10		◆			◆
11					◆
12					◆
13	◆		◆		
14	◆				
16	◆				
18	◆				
19	◆				
21	◆				
23	◆				
25	◆				
27	◆			◆	◆
29		◆			
31		◆			
33		◆			

PAGE	Number & Operations	Algebra	Geometry	Measurement	Data Analysis & Probability
35	◆			◆	
36	◆	◆			
37			◆		
39			◆		
41		◆	◆		
43			◆		
45				◆	◆
47				◆	
49				◆	
51	◆			◆	◆
52		◆		◆	
54	◆			◆	
56	◆			◆	
58	◆			◆	
60	◆	◆	◆	◆	

Source: National Council of Teachers of Mathematics. (2000). *Principles and standards for school mathematics.* Reston, VA: NCTM. www.nctm.org

Any Time Is Math Time

Use these quick activities to keep your children's minds on math at the beginning or end of class, as they are lining up to change classes, or any time you have a few minutes to fill.

1. COLOR ME BLUE

Have children use this simple classification activity as you call on them to line up. Call by colors: children wearing blue; children wearing red; children who have brown eyes; and so on.

2. CALENDAR MATH

Use your classroom calendar for math discussion. For example, ask:

◆ What is today's date? What will the date be tomorrow? What was the date yesterday? What will be the date two days from now?

◆ Read the number of today's date. For dates with two-digit numbers: What would the number be if we reversed the numerals? What place is the (2) in? What place is the (8) in?

3. KIDS' RULE!

Give examples of items children can find around the classroom and ask them whether a finger, hand, or foot would be easiest to use as a unit to measure each one. For example:

◆ the width of your crayon (finger)

◆ the length of your desk (hand)

◆ the distance from the front door of the school to the classroom (foot)

◆ the height of the door (hand)

◆ the length of your hair (finger or hand)

4. TIME FOR SCHOOL

Ask children to look at the clock and count with you to find out how many full hours they spend in school each day.

5. MISSING YOU

While taking attendance, ask questions such as:

◆ How many children are absent today?

◆ How many are present?

◆ (Point to one child.) How many children would there be in class today if you were absent?

◆ (Point to additional children.) How many children would be in class today if you and you were absent?

Any Time Is Math Time

More quick activities to keep children's minds on math...

6. IT TAKES TIME

Think of familiar activities. Ask children whether they would use seconds, minutes, or hours to measure these actions:

◆ eat a cookie (minutes)

◆ blink ten times (seconds)

◆ brush teeth (minutes)

◆ eat dinner (minutes)

◆ sleep all night (hours)

7. A MINUTE AND COUNTING

Ask children what number they think they can count to in one minute. As a class, have children count softly as you tell them when to start and stop counting. Change the amount of time to two minutes, three minutes, etc. Help the class estimate how long it would take them to count to 100.

8. STAND UP, SIT DOWN

Have children stand one at a time and count off, saying their own numbers. Then ask one child at a time to sit down. As they do, children count back.

9. TICK-TOCK

When the classroom clock is on an hour, ask children to tell you what time it is. What time will it be in one hour? in two hours? What time was it one hour ago?

10. WHAT A SQUARE!

Give each child a square piece of paper. Ask them to see how many ways they can fold it in half.

Classification Show-and-Tell

Turn Show-and-Tell time into a sorting and classifying activity.

PREPARATION
Ask each child to bring in a toy or stuffed animal for show-and-tell. Before show-and-tell time begins, set out several boxes or mark off areas in your room.

DIRECTIONS
1. Today is a special show-and-tell day! Tell children that as they show their toys, you would like the class to see if they can find toys that are alike in some way. Have children sort the first few toys into basic categories, for example, stuffed animals, toys with wheels, and games. As children continue to share their toys, have the class decide which group a new toy or game is most like. For example: If the toys sorted so far are a stuffed teddy bear, a car, and a board game, where would a puzzle of bears driving trucks go? Let children decide.

2. When all the toys have been placed in a category, review each member of the category. Show all the items that have been put together and see if children still agree that they belong together. Then ask the class to think of a label that will describe each category.

3. Display a subgroup of the toys and make some categories of your own. Ask children to find toys that fit your category. For example, you might gather a group of stuffed animals and ask children to find animals that are brown, animals that swim, animals that fly, and so on.

ASSESSMENT
Observe if children are able to identify different attributes and assign items to a group based on common attributes. If children offer categories such as "things I like," help them understand that this is not a good way to classify because others would not be able to follow the classification rule.

Grouping
Whole class

You'll Need
◆ Several large boxes (optional)

Teaching Tip

In this activity, no classification is wrong as long as children can justify their thinking.

Home Link

Inform families of this classifying activity. A fun way for children to clean up their play areas or their room is to have them pick up and put away items using classification. For instance: Pick up and put away all of your green toys. Pick up and put away all of your toys that make noise.

Old MacDonald Had a Farm

This familiar song theme makes a great "closing act" to this animal classification activity.

Grouping

Individual

You'll Need

For each child:

◆ Old MacDonald Had a Farm (reproducible page 11)

◆ Scissors

Teaching Tip

Students may have different explanations about why an animal does or doesn't belong in a group. No answer is wrong as long as it can be logically justified.

DIRECTIONS

1. Explain that children will help Farmer MacDonald group some of the animals on his farm. Distribute reproducible page 11 and ask children to cut out the animals. Ask them to make a group of some of the animals and be ready to tell the class why they put those animals together.

2. After several children have shown and explained their groups, tell children they'll use their animals to do a different kind of grouping activity. Tell them to use their pictures to show the groups of animals you call out. Explain that they should be ready to tell you which animal in your group doesn't belong and why. Groups you can use:

   ◆ cow, lamb, duck, goat (The duck does not belong because it has only two legs and all of the others have four; because it is the only one that can fly; because it has feathers.)

   ◆ chicken, duck, turkey, goat (The goat does not belong because all of the others have wings; because all of the others have feathers.)

   ◆ turkey, duck, chicken, rooster (The duck does not belong because it is the only one that can swim.)

3. At the end of the activity, sing a round of the song "Old MacDonald." Have children act out the roles of the farm animals. While everyone else sings the song, pick children to act like each animal and on cue make the sound their animal makes.

ASSESSMENT

See if children can identify several attributes of the animals and find a variety of ways to classify the groups. Can children express the rule being used?

VARIATION

Have children draw other animals and add them to the set to create their own grouping for classmates to guess.

Old MacDonald Had a Farm

Getting to Know You

Children create a class Venn diagram— and learn more about each other as they do.

Grouping

Whole class

You'll Need

◆ Removable sticky notes, one for each child

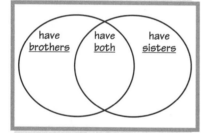

have brothers / have both / have sisters

Writing Connection

Help children write some questions they would like the class to answer.

PREPARATION

Draw two large intersecting circles on the chalkboard. Write the category you want to discuss in each circle.

DIRECTIONS

1. Tell children that they will share some information about themselves and make a "picture" to show it. Distribute a sticky note to each child and ask children to write their names on the notes.

2. Use a series of categories that can overlap. Each time, have children put their names in the circle that describes themselves. Categories to use include:

   ◆ have brothers/have sisters/have both brothers and sisters
   ◆ have a dog/have a cat/have both a dog and a cat
   ◆ walk to school/ride a bike to school/both walk and ride
   ◆ wear sneakers/wear shoes/wear both sneakers and shoes
   ◆ like chocolate ice cream/like vanilla ice cream/like both chocolate and vanilla equally well

3. As each Venn diagram is built, ask questions that require children to interpret the information. For example: Who has brothers? Who has sisters? Who has both? Who has neither? Are there more children in our class who have brothers or who have sisters? How many more? Children will quickly see why there is a need for an intersecting section on the "picture" for children who fit both conditions. As soon as the situation arises, ask the class to decide where sticky note names should go if children who fit none of the attributes.

ASSESSMENT

Listen to children's responses to see if they can interpret the information on the Venn diagram.

➤➤➤ EXTENSION

Use some of your categories again and make bar graphs of the results. Discuss the different ways the same information can be represented. Compare the Venn diagram to the bar graph. Ask children which one is easier to read and why.

Number Tour

Take your class on a walking tour of your school and discover the fun of finding numbers everywhere you look.

PREPARATION
Before doing the activity with your class, you may want to take a tour of your school in search of numbers.

DIRECTIONS
1. Explain to children that they'll be going on an indoor field trip—with you as the guide. On their tour, children will be looking for numbers, anywhere they can spot them! Start the tour in your classroom. Ask children to find numbers. Some likely and more obvious places are the clock and the calendar. See what other examples children can find and start your list of "Numbers We Found."

2. Have children line up with partners and take them on an orderly walk through the hallways past other classrooms, into the library, into the office, into the cafeteria, and so on. At each stop, remind children to be on the lookout for numbers.

3. When you're back in your classroom, complete your list of numbers and then discuss children's findings. For each citing on the list, ask children if they can tell the purpose the numbers serve. For example: numbers on the clock help us tell time; numbers on pages of a book help us find the page we want; numbers on classroom doors help children and visitors find the room they're looking for.

ASSESSMENT
See if children are able to find examples without your help. Note children who discover less obvious examples and those who can explain the purpose the numbers serve.

➡➡➡ EXTENSION
Draw a simple "map" of your school indicating the many math findings children discovered. Post the map on the bulletin board and use yarn or string to attach children's pictures or names to locations they found.

Grouping
Whole class

You'll Need
◆ Large piece of poster or chart paper
◆ Markers

Writing Connection

Have children choose one example of the numbers found on the walking tour and draw a picture or write about that use of numbers. Post pictures on a Number Tour bulletin board.

Name That Number!

Children match numerals and number words to complete this crossnumber puzzle.

Grouping

Individual

You'll Need

◆ Name That Number! (reproducible page 15), one copy for each child

◆ Pencils

Writing Connection

Use a recent classroom event to have children craft a number story. They should write about the event using some of the number words they've just practiced.

PREPARATION

Write the number words *one* through *ten* on the chalkboard.

DIRECTIONS

1. Review the number words *one* through *ten* by asking volunteers to read the words on the chalkboard. After each word is identified, ask another child to write the numeral next to it.

2. Distribute reproducible page 15 to each child. Draw attention to the number clues for the letters going across and the letters going down. Have children find and point to those letters on the crossnumber puzzle. Explain to children that they should use the clues to spell out number words in the spaces on the puzzle. One letter goes in each space. If they work carefully, they'll find a place for all of the numbers from one to ten!

ASSESSMENT

Be sure children understand how to put letters in the boxes to complete the puzzle. As they're working, move about the room and ask children to read some of the number words.

➔➔➔ EXTENSION

For more practice reading and writing numbers, help children create labels for items in the classroom, for example, *one* chair, *two* tables, *five* windows, and so on. Help children post their labels and have children quickly read them each morning for a few days.

Name That Number!

Follow the clues.
Write the word for each number.

ACROSS

B. 6

C. 7

E. 3

G. 4

I. 10

J. 2

DOWN

A. 5

D. 9

F. 8

H. 1

Counting Cows, Counting Sheep

With the help of Little Boy Blue, children represent numbers using manipulatives.

Grouping

Individual

You'll Need

◆ Several sets of class-room objects: books, pencils, pieces of chalk, etc.

For each child:

◆ **Counting Cows, Counting Sheep (reproducible page 17)**

◆ Five each of two different colored counters

DIRECTIONS

1. Show children a set of objects, for example, 5 books. Ask the class to count how many items there are. Show another set with a different number of objects, such as 3 pencils. Again ask children to tell how many there are. Then ask which group has more. Are there more books or more pencils? See if anyone can tell you how many more.

2. Repeat the activity with other groups of objects. As you ask children about the number of items, ask questions about *more, fewer,* and the *same amount.*

3. Distribute reproducible page 17 and counters to each child. Tell children that they are to use their counters to represent things as you give directions. Here are some examples:

   ◆ Little Boy Blue, come blow your horn. There are two sheep in the meadow and three cows in the corn.

   Ask children to put out two groups of counters to show the numbers. Then ask which group has more.

   ◆ Little Boy Blue, come blow your horn. There are five sheep in the meadow and four cows in the corn.

   Observe that children put out the correct number of counters. Then ask which group has fewer.

   ◆ Little Boy Blue, come blow your horn. There are more sheep in the meadow than cows in the corn.

   See if children can represent more sheep without a given number of cows.

✛✛✛ VARIATION

After children use the reproducible with their counters, have them finish by drawing some cows and sheep. As children show their pictures, the class can tell how many animals there are and talk about *more, fewer,* and *same amount.*

50+ Super-Fun Math Activities: Grade 1 © 2010 by Scholastic Inc.

Name

Counting Cows, Counting Sheep

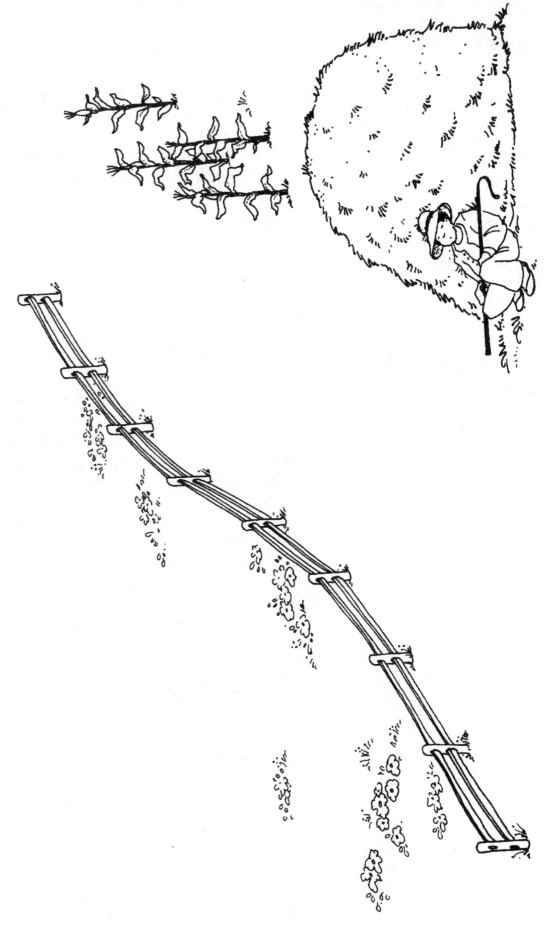

Line Up for Number Lines!

Mixed-up numbers are no problem as children put themselves in order to make a number line.

Grouping

Whole class

You'll Need

◆ Construction paper
◆ Markers

PREPARATION

Before class, make a large number on each piece of construction paper. Number until you reach the number of children in your class.

DIRECTIONS

1. Randomly give each child a number. To be sure they can identify their own numbers, call out each number in order and have the child with that number hold it up.

2. Call out the numbers from 1 to 10 and have those children come to the front of the classroom. Ask them to put themselves in order and hold up their number signs. When they are organized, have the class read the numbers and count from 1 to 10.

3. Have the remaining children come up and arrange themselves in order to complete the class number line. Count together from 1 to the last number. Ask children questions such as:

   ◆ Tara is number 14. What number comes before 14? What number comes after 14?

   ◆ Seth is the last number on our line. What's his number? What number would come after that?

4. Make number line patterns. For example, have every other child step forward. Have the front row count by 2s using their sequence (2, 4, 6, 8, etc.) and the back row count by 2s using their sequence (1, 3, 5, 7, etc.). Use other categories and have children step forward and say their number. For example: children with 0 in their number; children who have count-by-5 numbers; children who have numbers that end with -*teen*.

ASSESSMENT

For children having trouble identifying and ordering numbers, use a more limited set of numbers and have them practice naming the numbers and putting themselves in order.

✛✛✛ VARIATION

Have each child draw a self-portrait. When the pictures are complete, give each child a number and have him or her write it above the drawing. Have children hang up their portraits in numerical order in your classroom or in the hall.

Decorate Your Birthday Cake

Children add candles to the birthday cakes of their dreams.

DIRECTIONS

1. Ask children to show you various ways to represent how old they are. If most children are six or seven, how could they show six or seven? Invite as many responses as children can think of. They might write the numerals, hold up fingers, draw sticks, line up chairs, show counters, and so on.

2. Next, ask children to tell you how many candles they would put on a cake to represent their age. What if they were four? What if they were ten?

3. Distribute reproducible page 20 and help children read the "caption" in each of the four boxes. Tell them they should decorate each cake any way they wish and then draw candles on each one to show their age—in the past, now, and in the future.

ASSESSMENT

Observe if children are able to correlate age with the number of candles.

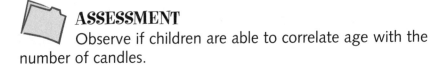 **EXTENSION**

Locate pictures in books and magazines of children with birthday cakes. Children might bring in pictures of themselves, friends, or siblings at birthday parties. Have children count the candles to determine the age of the birthday child in each picture.

 **Grouping**

Individual

You'll Need

For each child:

◆ **Decorate Your Birthday Cake (reproducible page 20)**

◆ Crayons

Name _____

Decorate Your Birthday Cake

My birthday cake
age 1

My birthday cake
age 3

My birthday cake
this year

My birthday cake
5 years from now

50+ Super-Fun Math Activities: Grade 1 © 2010 by Scholastic Inc.

Circus Seek and Find

**Children search the big top to answer
three-ring addition problems.**

DIRECTIONS

1. Tell children they'll use a picture to count and add. Distribute reproducible page 22 and counters to each child. Have volunteers identify the number of animals or performers in each ring.

2. Ask a series of addition questions. Have children put out counters for the animals or performers to help them count and add. Ask questions such as these:

   ◆ How many dancing dogs can you find in the top ring? How many dancing dogs are in the middle ring? How many dancing dogs are there altogether?

   ◆ How many clowns are there in the top ring? How many clowns are there in the middle ring? Which ring has more? How could you make the number the same?

   ◆ How many elephants are in the top ring? How many are in the middle ring? How many are in the bottom ring? How many elephants are there in all?

3. Once you've modeled some questions like those above, ask children to make up questions about the circus for their classmates to solve. After each child poses a question, give the rest of the class time to put out their counters and answer the question.

ASSESSMENT

Observe which children use their counters and count one by one to find the total. Which children are beginning to add without counting? Can children answer the questions without the counters?

⇥⇥⇥ EXTENSION

Write several addition sentences on the chalkboard to represent addition situations on reproducible page 22. Ask children to tell you which circus performers you are thinking of. For example, write

$$2 + 1 + 1 = 4$$

(This number sentence represents the number of clowns.)

Grouping

Individual

You'll Need

For each child:

◆ **Circus Seek and Find (reproducible page 22)**

◆ **15 counters**

Writing Connection

Have children write a number story about the circus scene.

21

Name _____

Circus Seek and Find

Addition Fact Adventures

Children travel on safari and play an addition game.

DIRECTIONS

1. Invite children to play an addition adventure game. They'll meet some "wild" addition problems along the way.

2. Distribute reproducible page 24, a pencil, and a paper clip to each group. Show children how to use the spinner by spinning a paper clip around the point of a pencil placed at the center of the spinner. Give each child a counter to use as a playing piece.

3. Explain the game moves. Children take turns using the spinner and moving that number of spaces. They can take shortcuts to reach the end: if a player lands on a shortcut, he or she should move across the bridge to the space with the star. The winner is the first player to land on (but not past) the 30 mark. Children should keep playing until all players have landed on 30.

4. After players in all the groups have reached the end, talk about the game. Ask questions such as these:

   ◆ If you are on 5 and you spin 2, what space will you move to?
   ◆ How many spaces do you skip if you land on 1?
   ◆ Which space would you move to if you land on 6? How many spaces do you skip?
   ◆ Which space is it most helpful to land on? Why?
   ◆ Which number did the spinner land on most often? Why do you think that happened?

ASSESSMENT
Observe if children are beginning to use addition strategies as well as counting as they move around the board.

➔➔➔ EXTENSION
Instead of the shortcut paths only moving players forward, use the circles and stars to direct players forward and backward. On index cards, write simple addition and subtraction problems for children to solve. When a player lands on a space with a circle or a star, he or she must pick a card and correctly solve the problem. If the player fails to give the correct answer, he or she either cannot take the shortcut forward (a player on a circle), or must take the "shortcut" backward (a player on a star).

Grouping
Pairs or small groups

You'll Need

For each pair or group:

◆ **Addition Fact Adventures (reproducible page 24)**
◆ Counters (one per player)
◆ Pencils
◆ Paper clips

Writing Connection

Have children write addition sentences that represent the shortcuts on the board game. For example: $1 + 2 = 3$; $6 + 3 = 9$.

Addition Fact Adventures

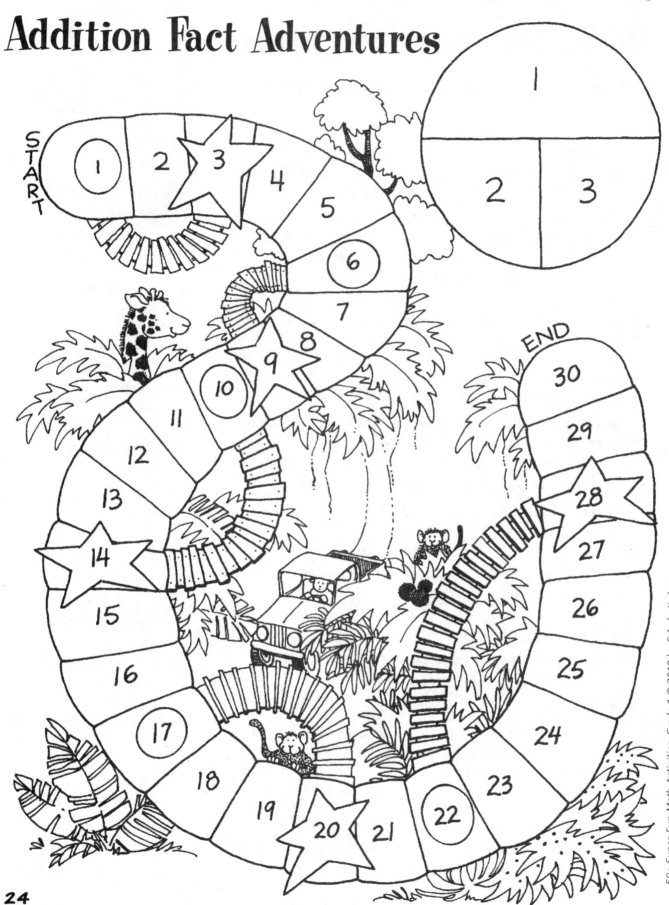

50+ Super-Fun Math Activities: Grade 1 © 2010 by Scholastic Inc.

Hansel and Gretel Subtraction

Children subtract counters to help Hansel and Gretel find their way through the woods and back home again.

DIRECTIONS

1. Read aloud this version of the Hansel and Gretel story:

Once upon a time, there were two children, a boy named Hansel and his sister, Gretel. One day the children decided to go for a walk in the woods. Gretel took along ten stones. To keep from getting lost, the children left a trail with the ten stones to mark their path.

When Hansel and Gretel had used the last of their ten stones, they found themselves at a house made of gingerbread, cakes, and candies. The children were so hungry that they began to eat the house. But the woman who lived there didn't like the idea of children eating her house! She told the children to go home.

Now Hansel and Gretel are trying to find their way home. They are having a hard time, because the woods are filled with stones just like the ones they left behind. Which path should they take? You can help.

2. Distribute reproducible page 26 and 10 counters to each pair. Explain that they should start at the gingerbread house and follow paths, taking away the number of counters shown on each stone. Children can move left, right, up, down, and diagonally to follow paths. Since Hansel and Gretel used all ten of their stones to get from their home to the gingerbread house, children must find paths that use exactly ten to get them home again.

3. After children have had a chance to try several paths, have pairs trace one of their paths and show it to the class. See how many different paths of ten children were able to find.

Grouping

Pairs

You'll Need

For each pair:

◆ Hansel and Gretel Subtraction (reproducible page 26)

◆ 10 counters

◆ Pencils

ASSESSMENT

See if children can figure out several paths that will use ten counters. Have the class check each path as it is shown to be sure it is exactly ten.

▶▶▶ EXTENSION

Ask children to find the paths that take the most and the fewest stones.

Hansel and Gretel Subtraction

START

2	1	1	1	1
1	1	2	3	1
1	1	3	2	1
1	2	1	1	1
1	1	1	1	2

STOP

50+ Super-Fun Math Activities: Grade 1 © 2010 by Scholastic Inc.

I'm Bigger Than You!

Children listen to an original math tale and use a bar graph of different critters' lengths to compare and subtract.

DIRECTIONS

1. Read "I'm Bigger Than You" to your class.

In a pond far away, the animals lived in peace. But the bullfrog, the spotted turtle, and the small salamander liked to tease the teeny, tiny cricket frog because she was so small.

One day, a snake came to the pond. Whenever he met another animal, he would sssay, "I'm bigger than you!"

After a few weeks, all of the animals got together to see if there was something they could do about this. They thought and thought. The cricket frog hopped up and was about to offer an idea, but the others said, "You're too little. We don't need little ideas from a little cricket frog."

While the animals talked about what they should do, the snake slithered up. "I'm bigger than you!" he sssaid to the salamander. "I'm bigger than you!" he ssspoke to the spotted turtle. "And I'm even bigger than you!" he hisssed at the bullfrog.

Just then, the cricket frog spoke up, "But you are not bigger than all of us put together!"

"I must be. You are all so very sssmall," sssneered the snake.

"If together we are bigger than you, we must all agree to live together peacefully," the cricket frog said.

The snake, confident that he would win, agreed. So the bullfrog, the spotted turtle, and the salamander lined up head-to-tail next to the snake. Now they were really confused! Together, they were just the same length as the snake. "Don't forget about me," called the cricket frog, as she hopped to the end of the line. "Now we're bigger than you," she said to the snake. And they were!

2. Divide the class into small groups and distribute reproducible page 28 and linking cubes. Read the story again and have children use the information on the bar graph to build each animal. Ask questions such as these, encouraging children to place cube animals on the bar graph if needed:

◆ How long is the bullfrog? How long is the cricket frog? How much longer is the bullfrog?

◆ How much longer is the snake than each of the other animals?

◆ How much shorter is the snake than the other animals together?

Grouping

Small groups

You'll Need

◆ **I'm Bigger Than You!** (reproducible page 28), one copy for each group

◆ 20 linking cubes

Writing Connection

Children can use the I'm Bigger Than You! graph and their cube animals to model addition and subtraction situations. Help children make up stories and record number sentences for their stories.

I'm Bigger Than You!

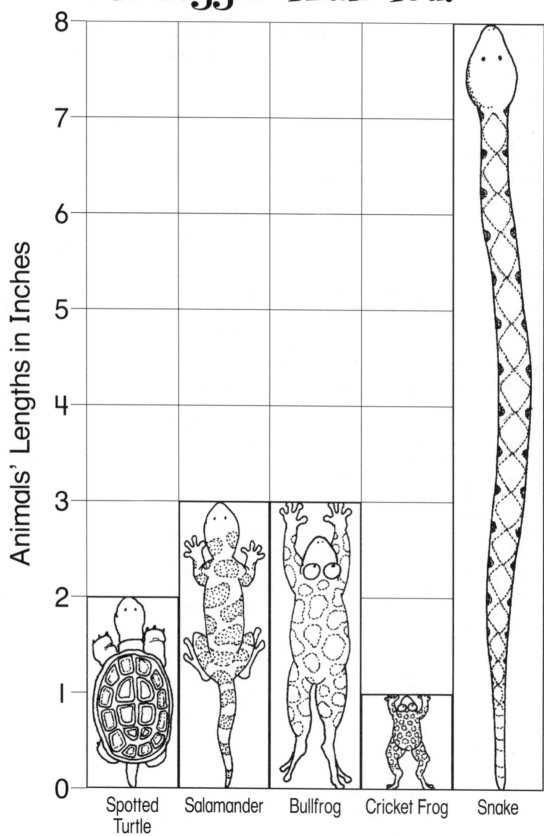

Animals' Lengths in Inches

8
7
6
5
4
3
2
1
0

Spotted Turtle   Salamander   Bullfrog   Cricket Frog   Snake

50+ Super-Fun Math Activities: Grade 1 © 2010 by Scholastic Inc.

String-Along Patterns

Children extend and create bead patterns.

DIRECTIONS

1. Show children a simple pattern of shapes or colors. Ask children to look around the classroom for other examples of patterns, such as patterns on clothing. If possible, make some bead patterns to show your class. You might make a pattern of all one color but different shapes, or a pattern that shows alternating colors. For each pattern, ask children to identify the pattern and tell what shape would come next.

2. Distribute reproducible page 30. If necessary, review the colors that each bead is labeled. Ask children to color the beads, decide what colors the unlabeled beads should be, and color them to complete the pattern. In the box, children should draw and color their own pattern.

3. When children have finished, review their work with the class. Ask volunteers to name the patterns and tell what comes next. Allow as many children as possible to show the patterns they made on their own.

Grouping

Individual

You'll Need

◆ **String-Along Patterns (reproducible page 30),** one copy for each child

◆ Red and blue crayons

◆ Real beads and string (optional)

ASSESSMENT

Look at children's work to see if they were able to continue a given pattern. Which children were able to create and describe their own patterns?

✦✦✦ VARIATIONS

◆ Use actual beads and let children string them to make patterns. Children can take turns showing and guessing one another's patterns.

◆ Use correction fluid to remove the color labels written on the beads, and write number patterns on the beads instead. For example: 1, 2, 1, 2; 2, 2, 1, 2, 2, 1. Have children complete the number patterns.

Name _____

String-Along Patterns

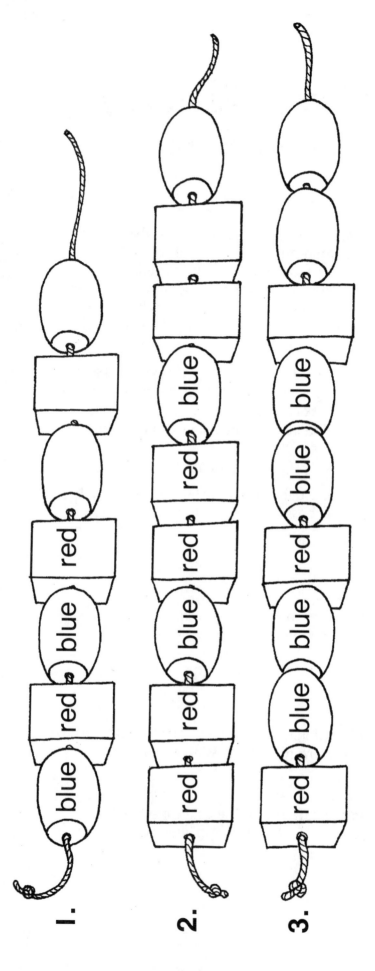

1.

2.

3.

4. Make up your own pattern. Draw it here.

Cereal Art Patterns

Children create beautiful cereal pictures while learning about patterns.

PREPARATION

Mix the three kinds of cereal together. Set out a small paper cup for each child and fill it with the cereal mix. Draw some simple shape and color patterns on the chalkboard or display them on an overhead projector.

DIRECTIONS

1. Show children the patterns you've prepared. Ask them to identify each pattern and tell you what shape or color would come next. If children have completed reproducible page 30, you might discuss some of the bead patterns children found.

2. Distribute reproducible page 32 and a cup of cereal to each child. Tell them that they will be gluing the cereal to their paper to make a cereal pattern. Remind them not to eat their art project!

3. Draw attention to the Key at the top of the page. Have children decide which color/shape cereal will represent the numbers on the pattern grid. Then tell them to glue that color/shape cereal to the Key. For example, a yellow piece of cereal could represent the number 1, so a yellow piece would be glued next to the number 1 in the Key. After children complete the Key, they can use it to make the pattern. For example, each time the number 1 appears on the pattern grid, a yellow piece of cereal would be glued on top of it.

4. When they are done and the cereal patterns are dry, have children share them with the class. Discuss the patterns that children made.

ASSESSMENT

See if children can use the Key and "translate" the shapes onto the numbered pattern grid. Do children keep the colors/shapes consistent or are they placing pieces of cereal randomly on the grid?

 Grouping

Individual

 You'll Need

◆ **Cereal Art Patterns (reproducible page 32),** one for each child

◆ Small paper cups

◆ Cereal mix that has three different shapes or colors

◆ Glue or paste

 Teaching Tip

If you think some children will have trouble interpreting the Key, work with that group and have the group decide on a Key they'll all use.

Cereal Art Patterns

KEY	
1 =	
2 =	
3 =	

1	1	1	1	1	1	1	1
1	2	2	2	2	2	2	1
1	2	3	3	3	3	2	1
1	2	3	1	1	3	2	1
1	2	3	1	1	3	2	1
1	2	3	3	3	3	2	1
1	2	2	2	2	2	2	1
1	1	1	1	1	1	1	1

50+ Super-Fun Math Activities: Grade 1 © 2010 by Scholastic Inc.

We Love Ice Cream!

Ice cream scoops are a "cool" way for children to learn about patterns.

PREPARATION
Make a transparency of reproducible page 34 and cut out the cone and scoops. Or make a cone and scoops out of construction paper.

DIRECTIONS
1. Display your own cone and scoops. Tell children that each scoop is a different flavor of ice cream. Ask the class to make suggestions for flavors. Begin with two flavors and fill your ice cream cone with a pattern of scoops. For example, you might show vanilla-chocolate-vanilla-chocolate. After you show two repetitions, ask children what flavor will come next.

2. Distribute reproducible page 34 to each pair. Have children cut out the cone and scoops of ice cream and color them in two colors of their choice. They might want to make unusual flavors such as grape (purple), orange (orange), blueberry (blue), chocolate chip (white with brown dots), etc. Remind them to make only two colors—each person of the pair can pick a color (flavor). They should then cut out the cone and scoops.

3. Tell pairs to take turns arranging scoops on top of the cone to create a pattern and guessing what will come next in the pattern.

ASSESSMENT
See which children can successfully create patterns without your help.

 EXTENSION
On the chalkboard, list all of the different patterns children found. Ask each pair to choose one of their patterns to represent. Tell them to glue their pattern onto a piece of construction paper to display on a We Love Ice Cream bulletin board.

 Grouping
Pairs

 You'll Need

- **We Love Ice Cream! (reproducible page 34),** one copy for each pair
- Crayons
- Scissors
- Glue or paste (optional)

Writing Connection

In their math journals, tell children to draw pictures to record as many combinations of scoops as they can find. Help them write the patterns using color words.

Name _____

We Love Ice Cream!

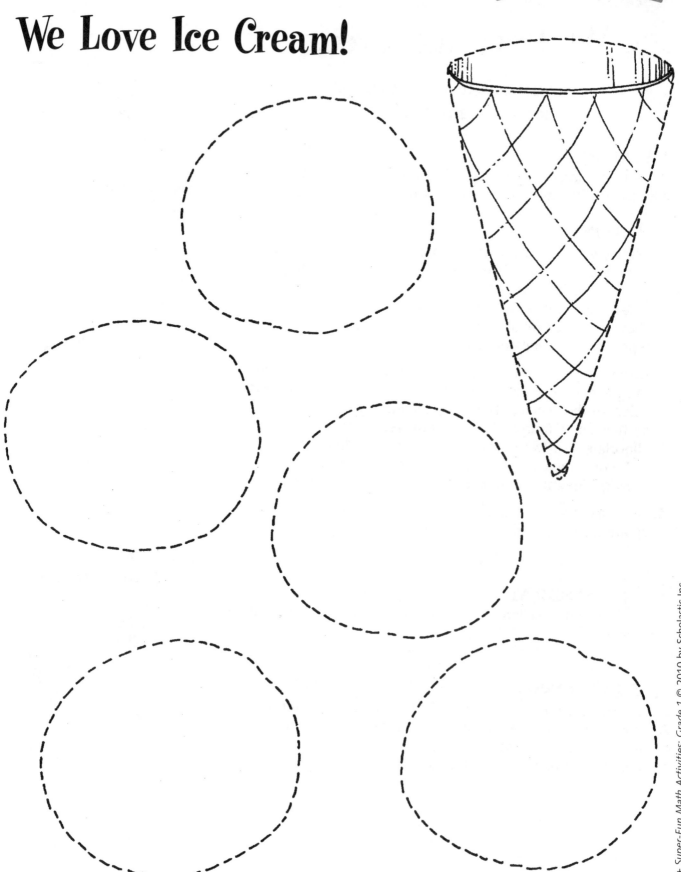

50+ Super-Fun Math Activities: Grade 1 © 2010 by Scholastic Inc.

Problems and More

Here are some problems you can pose to children. On the next page, and on page 60, are reproducibles with problems children can tackle on their own.

1. DOG BITES

If you were eating a foot-long hot dog and you took one-inch bites, how many bites would it take to finish it?

2. ADDITION AND THE THREE BEARS

◆ If the three bears invited the three little pigs for porridge, how many bowls of porridge would be needed?

◆ If Goldilocks and the three bears invited the three little pigs for porridge, how many bowls of porridge would be needed?

3. MONEY IN YOUR HAND

If you had a penny for each finger of your hand, how many pennies would you have? How much money would you have? (Ask this riddle with nickels, dimes, and quarters also.)

4. TELLING TALES

Listen to the name of each story. Tell the number words.

Snow White and the Seven Dwarfs
Three Billy Goats Gruff
The Five Chinese Brothers
The Three Little Pigs
Goldilocks and the Three Bears
One White Sail

Do you know other stories with number words?

5. MAKING TEN

Give classroom situations and have children add up to 10. For example:

◆ Three children are in the reading corner. How many more need to join them to make 10?

◆ Five children are at the math center. How many more need to join them to make 10?

6. PROBLEMS WITHOUT NUMBERS

Give some numberless problems and ask children whether they would add or subtract to find the answers. For example:

◆ Mark had some books. He got some more. How many did Mark have then?

◆ Luisa had some stickers. She gave some away. How many did she have left?

◆ Nina collected some shells. She lost some. How many did she have then?

Name _____

Problems and More

Put on your thinking cap to solve these problems!

1. Line Up Numbers

Draw straight lines. Make the sums.

4	6	5
3	2	1
3	1	2

Make 8

2	4	5
6	5	1
2	1	3

Make 10

5	1	3
2	6	4
3	2	5

Make 12

2. We're Hiding

Each group has 10 dots. How many are hidden?

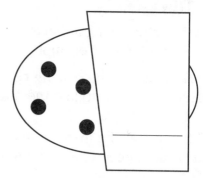 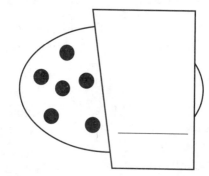 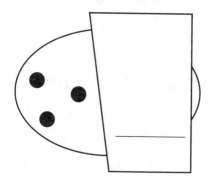

3. Make the Number

Circle numbers to make each sum.

7

2   1
5 3
      6

11

5   1
  3
2 9 6

14

6 2 9
1 4
     3

Did you find more than one way?

50+ Super-Fun Math Activities: Grade 1 © 2010 by Scholastic Inc.

Answers on page 64.

Let's Face It!

Children use different shapes to create a funny or unusual face.

DIRECTIONS

1. Many children have seen or made jack-o'-lanterns. Shapes such as circles, diamonds, and triangles are often used to create the features. Ask children what shapes they would use to make a jack-o'-lantern face. Offer these suggestions: circles, squares, triangles, diamonds, rectangles.

2. Distribute reproducible page 38 and scissors. Have children name the shapes. Next, tell children they should cut out the shapes and make a funny or unusual face. Invite children to show the face they made and tell about the shapes they used.

3. Sing or chant a shape song! Use the modified lyrics to the song "Aiken Drum." Start the chant and then use children's shape faces to invent additional verses of the chant. Hold up a child's picture as you create a verse.

> **There was a man, lived in the moon,**
> **Lived in the moon, lived in the moon,**
> **There was a man, lived in the moon,**
> **And his name was Aiken Drum.**
>
> **And he played upon a ladle, a ladle, a ladle,**
> **And he played up on a ladle, and his name was Aiken Drum.**

Now hold up one child's shape face.

> **And his eyes were made of circles, circles, circles,**
> **And his nose was make of triangles,**
> **And his name was Aiken Drum.**

Modify other verses according to children's pictures.

> **And his mouth was made of (squares).**
> **And his ears were made of (rectangles).**
> **And his eyes were made of (diamonds).**

Invite children to sing or chant along!

ASSESSMENT

Ask children to identify the different shapes they used to make a face. Can they point to a shape when you name it?

Grouping

Individual

You'll Need

◆ **Let's Face It! (reproducible page 38),** one copy for each child
◆ Scissors
◆ Glue or paste

Writing Connection

Have children label the shapes on the face they made.

Let's Face It!

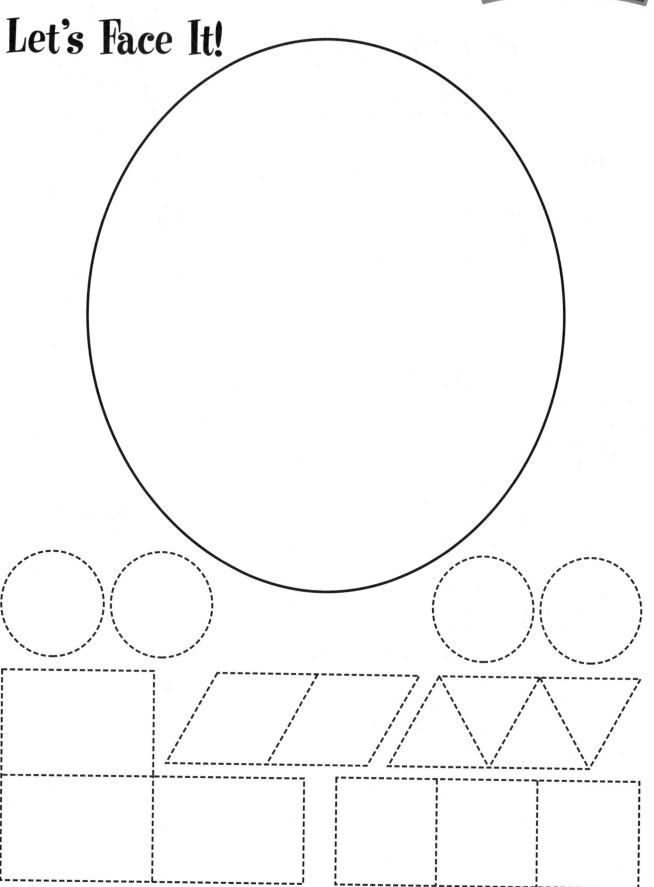

50+ Super-Fun Math Activities: Grade 1 © 2010 by Scholastic Inc.

Stars Take Shape

Children connect the stars to form constellations in this starry sky.

DIRECTIONS

1. Invite children to journey with you to Mathematica, a land not far from North America. When the people of Mathematica look up at the night sky they see groups of stars. They imagine that the stars form shapes, and they name each group of stars after things they think the stars look like.

2. Distribute reproducible page 40 and ask children to find the shapes the people of Mathematica see. (triangle, pinwheel, house) Ask children to draw straight lines to connect stars (dots) and re-create these constellation shapes. In the last box on the reproducible, ask children to invent their own star shape.

3. When children are finished, have them compare shapes with a friend. Then invite each child to share his or her own star shape with the class.

➔➔➔ EXTENSIONS

◆ Many wonderful stories and myths have been created about the constellations. One picture book, inspired by a Chinese legend about the stars, is Jennifer Armstrong's *Wan Hu Is in the Stars*.

◆ Have children use geoboards and rubber bands to make as many shapes as they can imagine. You can give them some ideas and then set them loose to make up their own!

Grouping

Individual

You'll Need

◆ **Stars Take Shape (reproducible page 40),** one copy for each child

◆ Pencils

◆ Geoboards and rubber bands (optional)

Name _____

Stars Take Shape

Make the shapes.

Make your own.

40

Tantalizing Tangrams

With tangrams, children can name geometric shapes—and make some shapes of their own.

DIRECTIONS

1. Explain to children that they'll be making a special kind of shape puzzle, called a tangram. Distribute reproducible page 42. Have children cut out the large square and then cut along the dashed lines to make seven separate pieces.

2. Invite children to find and name shapes they know. Children should be able to identify large and small triangles, and a square. If children ask, tell them that the remaining shape is called a parallelogram.

3. Now have children mix up the pieces of their tangrams. Ask them to use the pieces in any way they like to make new shapes. They can use some of the pieces or all of the pieces. Encourage children to show one another, or the class, the shapes they've made.

4. For a final challenge, ask children to see if they can put all the pieces of the puzzle back together again. What shape did the puzzle make? *(a large square)*

 **ASSESSMENT**

See if children can name the shapes that make up the square. If children are having difficulty re-forming the large square, show them an uncut tangram reproducible and see if they can match the pieces.

⇥⇥⇥ EXTENSION

Read *Grandfather Tang's Story*, or share Sam Loyd's *Book of Tangram Puzzles*. Invite children to use their tangram pieces to make the shapes described in these books.

 Grouping

Individual

 You'll Need

◆ **Tantalizing Tangrams (reproducible page 42),** one for each student
◆ Scissors

 Writing Connection

Invite children to draw and name a shape puzzle of their own. When they've made up a name, help them write it.

Tantalizing Tangrams

Cut out the tangram pieces.

Use the pieces to make shapes.

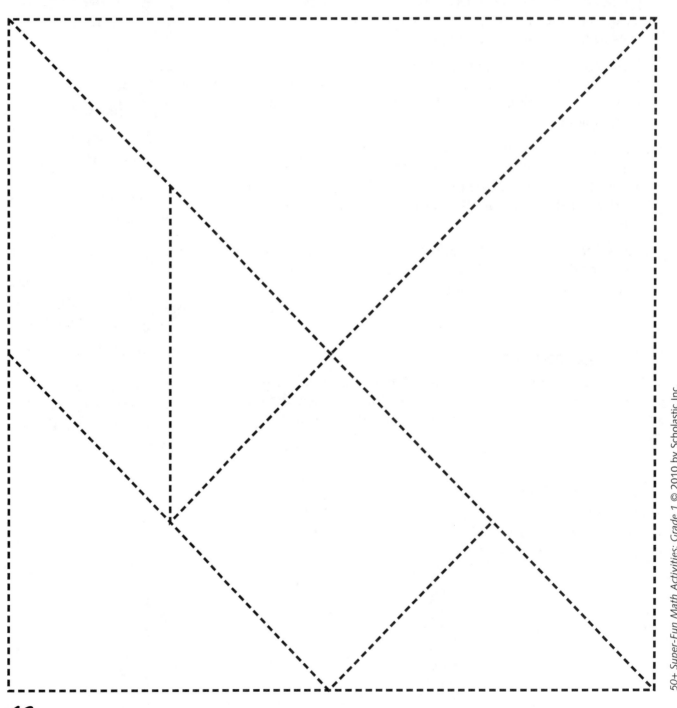

From Here to There

Children make their way around an amusement park and find out just how much fun map reading can be.

DIRECTIONS

1. Invite children to find their way around an amusement park—using a map! Have children choose partners, or divide the group into pairs. Distribute reproducible page 44 and crayons to each pair. Explain how to read the grid on a map: numbers show rows across and letters show columns up and down. Where a row and column meet, there is a square that locates parts of the amusement park.

2. Ask children to locate the following spots on the map and tell you what they would find there: 3C; 4E; 6G. Next have pairs take turns locating spots using the map grid and recording what they find.

3. Children can use crayons to trace paths from place to place in the amusement park. They should go only up or down, to the left or right. Give directions such as these, pausing after each one to allow children to trace the path they would follow:

   ◆ Start at the Lost and Found. Go to the ice cream booth.
   ◆ Start at the Teacup Ride. Go to the Ferris Wheel.

   After each path is drawn, ask volunteers to describe the path they took, using direction words, for example, "I went up 2 spaces and to the right 3 spaces." Discuss if there is more than one possible path to take.

ASSESSMENT

Observe if children can follow rows and columns to locate a particular square on the grid. Children should be able to use direction words to describe the paths they follow to get from one place to another.

➤➤➤ EXTENSION

Use inch grid paper to make a simple map of your classroom. Do the activity by having children locate paths in the classroom and then finding the same path on the map.

Grouping

Pairs

You'll Need

◆ **From Here to There (reproducible page 44),** one copy for each pair
◆ Crayons

Teaching Tip

You can make a transparency from reproducible page 44. Use that to locate a few places on the grid so that everyone can see how to read it.

Name _____

From Here to There

Write what
is at each place.

6B _____

2G _____

5E _____

	A	B	C	D	E	F	G	H
1		Bumper Cars		Petting Zoo			ROLLER COASTER	Swing Ride
2		Merry-Go-Round					Ferris Wheel	
3			Teacup Ride		POPCORN			
4			Boat Ride		Ice Cream			
5		Lost & Found			Hot Dogs	JUICE		
6	TICKETS						Coin Toss	

Birthday Calendar

Counting past 30? It's no problem when children are finding birthdays on a calendar.

DIRECTIONS

1. Show a calendar from the current month so children can identify the day of the week on which the month begins. Have children read with you as you point to the days of the week across the top of the calendar.

2. Divide the class into 12 groups and assign each group a month. Distribute reproducible page 46 to each group and have them label their month at the top. You will have to tell each group which day their month starts on—that's where they should write the number 1. Then have children number on from there to 28 (or 29), 30, or 31.

3. Now gather birthday information as a class. Have each child tell the date of his or her birthday. The groups must listen carefully! It's their job to write classmates' names on the dates that fall in their month.

4. When the calendars are completed, hang them up for the class to enjoy. Ask children questions about the information they see. What day of the week is (Rhonda's) birthday? Which month has most birthdays? Is there any month in which no one has a birthday? Do any children have the same birthday?

➡➡➡ EXTENSIONS

◆ After all the months are completed, display them along the chalkboard in mixed-up sequence. Ask children to put the year in order.

◆ Make a birthday bar graph. Write the months along the vertical axis and have children post sticky notes with their names across the row that shows their birthday. Talk with children about the information on the graph.

Grouping

12 groups

You'll Need

◆ **Birthday Calendar (reproducible page 46),** one copy for each group
◆ Pencils, crayons, or markers
◆ Calendar pages with all the months of the current year

Home Link

Ask children to talk with someone at home about special days and holidays. Share the events as a class and then record the events on the class calendar.

Birthday Calendar: _____

SUNDAY	MONDAY	TUESDAY	WEDNESDAY	THURSDAY	FRIDAY	SATURDAY

Time for Alice in Wonderland

This mixed-up series of pictures can be put in order to tell a story of Alice and the White Rabbit.

DIRECTIONS

1. "I'm late, I'm late, for a very important date!" Explain to children that in the story of Alice in Wonderland, Alice's friend the White Rabbit is always worried about the time. So that he won't be late, children can help him tell time and organize his day.

2. If necessary, review telling time to the hour. Use a demonstration clock if one is available, to show various times. Ask children to identify the time.

3. Distribute reproducible page 48 and scissors. Tell children that the pictures will tell a story of the White Rabbit's day with Alice. But the pictures are all mixed up. Have children cut the pictures along the dotted lines and then move the pictures around so that the story events occur in the correct order. The time on each clock should help children organize the story sequence.

4. When children are finished, ask them to retell the picture story and read the time shown on each clock.

ASSESSMENT

Note whether children are able to use both clues—the time on the clock and the logic of the story—to put the pictures in correct sequential order. Can the children see the correlation between the time on the clock and the events occurring in each picture?
Answers: Times in order should show 7:00, 9:00, 9:30, 2:30, 4:00, 4:30.

➔➔➔ EXTENSIONS

◆ Ask children to tell how much time has elapsed between the times in different pairs of pictures.

◆ Read a children's adaptation of *Alice in Wonderland* to the class. The Golden Book classic is a good example.

Grouping

Individual

You'll Need

◆ **Time for Alice in Wonderland (reproducible page 48),** one copy for each child

◆ Scissors

◆ Demonstration clock (optional)

Name _____

Time for Alice in Wonderland

Tick-Tock-Toe Bingo

Children write and tell time on digital and analog clocks while playing this "time-honored" game of Bingo.

PREPARATION
Write the digital and analog times for one o'clock to twelve o'clock on the chalkboard. Then write the times again on small pieces of paper and put the pieces in a bag or container.

DIRECTIONS

1. Refer to the times you've written on the chalkboard and ask children to read them. Then invite children to play a bingo time game.

2. Distribute reproducible page 50. Point out that times are missing in several places. Tell players to fill in any times they like, with a different time in each blank space. They should use only times to the hour. Check that children have all finished filling out the cards before you begin the game.

3. Give 15 counters to each child. Explain that you'll say a time, and children should use a counter to cover up the time you say on their bingo cards. The object of the game is to get five counters in a row, going down, across, or on the diagonal. The twist in this bingo game is that when you say a time, children can put a counter over any space that shows that time. When a player gets 5 in a row, she or he should call out, "Tick-Tock-Toe Bingo!"

4. One at a time, draw pieces of paper from your bag and read the time. Leave the drawn pieces out so you can keep track of the times you've called. When one child has called bingo, check the times. Then have children clear their boards, put the papers with times back in the bag, and play again.

ASSESSMENT
Observe as children prepare their boards and play to see if they can write and read both digital and analog times correctly. Note children who find times randomly as you call them and those who are more strategic in finding times that will be helpful in building five in a row.

Grouping
Whole class

You'll Need

◆ **Tick-Tock-Toe Bingo (reproducible page 50),** one for each child

◆ Small paper bag or container

◆ Counters (15 for each child)

◆ Pencils

Tick-Tock-Toe Bingo

(clock 12:00)	(clock 12:10)	8:00	(clock 8:45)	(clock 12:20)
1:00	:	(clock 12:05)	(clock 12:35)	(clock 12:00)
(clock 11:50)	9:00	**FREE SPACE**	:	3:00
2:00	(clock 12:00)	:	(clock 12:30)	11:00
(clock 12:25)	12:00	(clock 12:15)	6:00	(clock 10:50)

50+ Super-Fun Math Activities: Grade 1 © 2010 by Scholastic Inc.

Every Penny Counts!

As children estimate and count pennies. They can also collect money for a good cause.

PREPARATION
You may want to research several charitable organizations to which your class could contribute their pennies. If you plan on having children roll pennies, drop by the bank for penny rolls.

DIRECTIONS

1. Give a real or play penny to each child. Have them drop their pennies, one by one, in the penny jar. Count aloud together as the pennies are put in. How much money is there? Hold the jar so all can see and ask children to take a guess as to how many more times they'd have to put pennies in to fill the jar. Then how much money do they think there would be? Write their estimates. Each day, have children put in pennies until the jar is full. Keep track of the number of days and amounts of money.

2. You can make this a fund-raising activity by having children contribute real pennies each day until the jar is full. Talk with children about the organization they will collect pennies for. Here are some ideas for fund-raising on a small scale:

   ◆ Borrow a video. Show the video during recess or at lunch and ask viewers each to contribute a penny.

   ◆ Have your class put on a skit, perhaps one that explains the need for the organization you will contribute to. Invite families and other classes. Ask for penny donations at the performance.

   ◆ Organize a walkathon where contributors sign up to pay one penny per lap (around the schoolyard).

   As pennies are collected, do some money math with children. For example, find the new total each day. Make a thermometer graph, perhaps marked in increments of 50 cents, and track progress until a goal is reached. Use penny rolls to count out sets of 50 pennies.

Grouping
Whole class

You'll Need

◆ At least one penny for each child

◆ Glass pint jar

◆ Play pennies or counters (optional)

Writing Connection

Children can write letters to the charitable organization, local newspaper, principal, and families describing their fund drive.

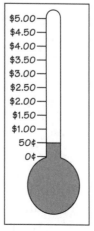

$5.00
$4.50
$4.00
$3.50
$3.00
$2.50
$2.00
$1.50
$1.00
50¢
0¢

Grouping

Pairs

You'll Need

For each pair:

◆ **Money Match-Up (reproducible page 53)**

◆ 20 sticky notes or small squares of dark paper

◆ Pencils

Money Match-Up

A nickel is the same as five pennies. Children find equivalent amounts of money in this money memory game.

PREPARATION

If sticky notes are not available, cut small squares of dark paper. Cut the paper so one piece will cover one square on the game board.

DIRECTIONS

1. Before children play the game, remind them that:
   ◆ a nickel equals 5 pennies
   ◆ a dime equals 2 nickels or 10 pennies
   ◆ a quarter equals 5 nickels, 2 dimes and 1 nickel, or 25 pennies

2. Have children choose partners or assign pairs. Distribute reproducible page 53 and sticky notes. Ask children to study the game board to see the money amounts that are shown. Then have them cover each box with a sticky note or paper square.

3. Explain that the object of the game is to collect sticky notes by matching equal amounts of money. The first player removes two notes. If the money amounts are equivalent, he or she keeps the notes. If they are not, the notes go back on the board to hide the money and the other player takes a turn. Children play in turn until all the sticky notes are removed. The player with the most notes wins.

4. Talk about how the game was played. Encourage children to share their strategies for finding equivalent amounts of money.

ASSESSMENT

As children play the game, note their ability to match amounts of money correctly. Although there is an element of visual memory involved in winning the game, the object is to provide practice identifying the different coin amounts and matching equivalents.

➤➤➤ EXTENSION

Give players 10 counters each. Each player should have a different color. As they make matches during the game, have them replace the sticky notes with their counters. At the end of the game, tell players to count the monetary value of their matches and find a total amount. The player with the higher total wins.

Money

Money Match-Up

25¢		**1¢**	
10¢			
5¢	**1¢**	**25¢**	**5¢**
			**10¢**

The Truth About the Tooth Fairy

When Ali Gator looses her teeth, how much money does the tooth fairy bring? Children add coin values to find out.

Grouping

Small groups

You'll Need

◆ **The Truth About the Tooth Fairy (reproducible page 55),** one copy for each group
◆ Play money
◆ Pencils

Writing Connection

Name an amount of money, such as 65 cents. If the tooth fairy left Ali that amount of money, which teeth might Ali have lost? Ask children to write or draw a picture to explain.

DIRECTIONS

1. Read this rhyme aloud:

   When Ali lost a tooth one day,
   The tooth fairy came to her to say,
   "You'll get a quarter for this tooth.
   But I must tell you the whole truth.
   Other teeth are worth a nickel, dime, or penny,
   Look at the picture to see just how many."

2. Distribute reproducible page 55 and play coins. Have children answer questions such as those below, using the picture of Ali Gator's teeth. Children can put out coins for each situation to help them determine the amounts of money. Encourage groups to figure out each answer together.

   ◆ How many teeth are worth a nickel?
   ◆ If Ali lost all of her teeth worth 5¢, how much money would she get?
   ◆ Look at Ali's top jaw. If Ali lost her two back teeth, how much would she get?
   ◆ Which coin would Ali get most often?
   ◆ What if Ali lost all her teeth. How much money would she get?

3. Have group members work together to complete the activity.

ASSESSMENT

See what techniques children are using to find the total amounts of money. Some children may use skip counting; others may "just know," for example, that two quarters are worth 50 cents.

▶▶▶ EXTENSION

Make a graph with children's names. Throughout the school year, when a child loses a tooth, post a tooth on the graph next to his or her name. At the end of the year, who has lost the most teeth? Is there a typical number of teeth lost by first graders? What else can children learn from the information on the graph?

Name _____

The Truth About the Tooth Fairy

Look at Ali Gator's teeth.

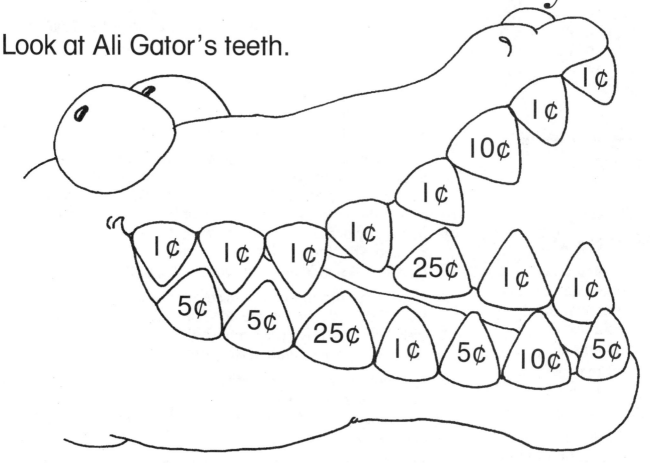

How many teeth?   How much money in all?

1. How many 1¢? [ ]   [ ] cents

2. How many 5¢? [ ]   [ ] cents

3. How many 10¢? [ ]   [ ] cents

4. How many 25¢? [ ]   [ ] cents

50+ Super-Fun Math Activities: Grade 1 © 2010 by Scholastic Inc.

Adding Weight

This simple scale activity helps children estimate and measure to see how much things weigh.

Grouping

Pairs

You'll Need

◆ **Adding Weight (reproducible page 57),** one copy for each pair

◆ Simple balance scale (or to make your own, see below)

◆ Dried beans

◆ Small, lightweight objects (must fit in pan of scale or cup)

◆ Pencils

DIRECTIONS

1. Explain to children that you want to see how heavy some things are. They will help you use beans to find the weight.

2. Divide your class into pairs and distribute reproducible page 57. Show children the columns for Object, Guess, and Real Weight. Display one object, such as a piece of chalk, and put it on one side of the scale. Show children your beans. Ask them to guess how many beans will equal the weight of the chalk. Have children write the word *chalk* (or draw a picture) and record their guess. Pairs should agree or take turns guessing.

3. Now put beans on the other side of the scale, one at a time. Have the class count as you add one bean at a time until the scale balances. Have children record the actual weight in beans. Talk about how accurate their guesses were.

4. Continue the activity with other small objects. Challenge children to think of ways they could get better at guessing the number of beans more accurately. For example, children might suggest holding two objects to compare them.

5. After several rounds of guess and check, discuss the results with children. Ask them to share their strategies for guessing. Talk about how children decide whether one object will be lighter (or heavier) than another object.

ASSESSMENT

Listen to children's strategies for guessing close to the actual number of beans. They should realize that size is not always a good indicator of weight.

TO MAKE A SCALE

Use string to suspend a paper cup from each arm of a hanger. (Hangers from children's clothing or lingerie work well.) Hang the scale in a place where the cups dangle freely without bumping into anything.

▶▶▶ EXTENSION

Place the scale and beans in your math center. Put out new objects to be weighed each week, or allow children to suggest them. The weight of coins would be interesting. Provide more copies of reproducible page 57 for children to record their findings.

Adding Weight

OBJECT	GUESS	REAL WEIGHT

High-Flying Measurement

Children use measurement to return fly-away kites to their owners.

Grouping

Individual

You'll Need

◆ High-Flying Measurement (reproducible page 59), one copy for each child

◆ Inch rulers

◆ Pencils or crayons

DIRECTIONS

1. Tell the class that some children lost their kites when the strings were broken. If they can find the right measurements, they can help the children get their kites back.

2. Distribute reproducible page 59. Explain that the number written on each kite tells the length in inches of its broken string. Ask children to guess which kite belongs to each child. Then distribute rulers and ask children to measure from the tip of each kite to the dot at the tip of each child's outstretched arm. When they find the right number of inches between a kite and a child, they can draw a string to reconnect that kite to its owner.

3. When children are finished, talk together about the results. Did everyone find the same answers? If not, ask children to measure again. Then ask children to look at their completed reproducibles and compare distances. Which kite is flying farthest from its owner? Which kite is closest? How do we know?

ASSESSMENT

Observe if children are placing and then reading the ruler correctly. Give assistance if necessary.

►►► EXTENSION

Have a high-flying paper airplane day! Help each child make a simple paper airplane. Take your class outside to fly the planes. From a set starting line, have each child fly his or her plane at least two times. Use a tape measure to determine the distances the planes flew. Record the distances and compare the two tries.

High-Flying Measurement

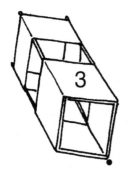

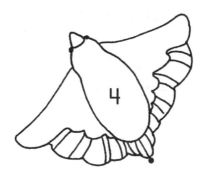

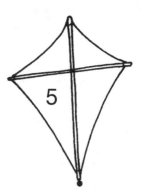

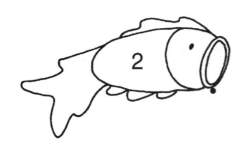

Name _____

Problems and More

Put on your thinking cap to solve these problems!

1. Alphabetical Order

Write the missing letters.

A, ☐ , C, ☐ , E, ☐ , G, ☐ , I, ☐ , K, ☐ , M, ☐ ,

O, ☐ , Q, ☐ , S, ☐ , U, ☐ , W, ☐ , Y, ☐

Make up your own letter pattern.
Have a friend fill in the missing letters.

2. Getting A-round to a Riddle

A zero, doughnut, ball, and grape,
are some things that have my shape.
What am I?
Draw the answer.

3. Sandwich Slices

Cut this sandwich so two friends
can have equal shares.

4. Making Money

Find 5 ways to make 25 cents.
Draw or write your ways on the back of this page.

50+ Super-Fun Math Activities: Grade 1 © 2010 by Scholastic Inc.

Answers on page 64.

An Assessment Toolkit

Alternative methods of assessment provide a comprehensive profile for each child. As children work on the activities in *50+ Super-Fun Math Activities: Grade 1*, here are some ways you might observe and record their work. Alone or in combination, they can provide a quick snapshot that adds to your knowledge of children's development in mathematics. They also give you concrete observations to share with families at reporting time.

FILE CARDS

An alphabetical file system, with a card for each child, provides a handy way to keep notes on children's progress. Choose a few children each day that you plan to observe. Pull their cards, jot down the date and activity, and record comments about their work.

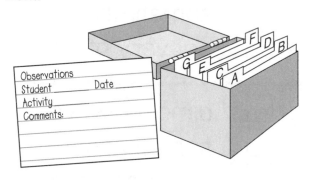

CLIPBOARDS

With a list of children attached to your clipboard, you can easily move about the classroom and jot down observations about their work and their thinking. If you want to focus on a particular skill or competency, you can create a quick checklist and simply check as you observe.

STICKY NOTES

As you circulate while individuals or small groups are working, create a sticky note for children who show particular strengths or areas for your attention and help. Be sure to date the note. The advantage to this technique is that you can move the notes to a record folder to create a profile; you can also cluster children with similar competencies as a reminder for later grouping.

CHECKLISTS AND RUBRICS

On pages 62 and 63, you'll find a few ready-made checklists and a rubric. Feel free to modify them to suit your own needs. Invite children to assess their own work—they are honest and insightful, and you'll have another perspective on their mathematical development!

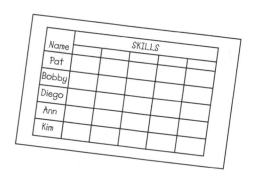

Self-Evaluation Form

ACTIVITY _____

---

1. I listened to directions...
☐ ... almost always
☐ ... sometimes
☐ ... not very often

---

2. I followed directions...
☐ ... almost always
☐ ... sometimes
☐ ... not very often

---

3. I could do the mathematics...
☐ ... almost always
☐ ... sometimes
☐ ... not very often

---

4. I could explain my work...
☐ ... almost always
☐ ... sometimes
☐ ... not very often

---

5. I worked with my group...
☐ ... almost always
☐ ... sometimes
☐ ... not very often

Assessment Checklist

Activity _____   Date _____   Group _____

Students					
MATHEMATICS KNOWLEDGE					
Understands problem or task					
Formulates and carries out a plan					
Explains concepts clearly					
Uses models or tools appropriately					
Makes connections to similar problems					
Can create similar problems					
MATHEMATICAL PROCESSES					
Justifies responses logically					
Listens carefully to others and evaluates information					
Reflects on and explains procedures					
LEARNING DISPOSITIONS					
Tackles difficult tasks					
Perseveres					
Shows confidence in own ability					
Collaborates/shares ideas					

50+ Super-Fun Math Activities: Grade 1 © 2010 by Scholastic Inc.

SCORING RUBRIC

3 Fully accomplishes the task

Shows full understanding of the central mathematical idea(s)

Communicates thinking clearly using oral explanation or written, symbolic, or visual means

2 Partially accomplishes the task

Shows partial understanding of the central mathematical idea(s)

Written or oral explanation partially communicates thinking, but may be incomplete, misdirected, or not clearly presented

1 Does not accomplish the task

Shows little or no grasp of the central mathematical idea(s)

Recorded work or oral explanation is fragmented and not understandable

Answers to Problems and More

PAGE 35

1. 12 bites

2. 6 bowls; 7 bowls

3. 5 pennies; 5 cents
   5 nickels; 25 cents
   5 dimes; 50 cents
   5 quarters; one dollar and 25 cents

4. Children should give number words.

5. 7 more; 5 more

6. add; subtract; subtract

PAGE 36

1.

4	6	5
3	2	
3	1	2

2	4	5
6	5	1
2		3

5	1	3
2	6	1
3	2	5

2. 6; 4; 7

3. 7 = 5 + 2, 6 + 1
   11 = 9 + 2, 6 + 3 + 2, 5 + 3 + 2 + 1, 6 + 5
   14 = 9 + 1 + 4, 2 + 3 + 9, 4 + 1 + 6 + 3
   (Addends can be in any order to make
   each sum.)

PAGE 60

1. Children should fill in the missing letters.

2. a circle

3.

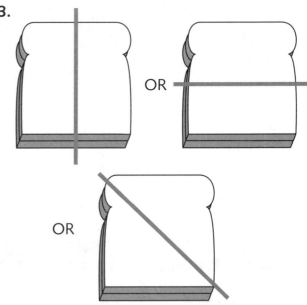

OR

OR

4. 1 quarter
   25 pennies
   20 pennies + 1 nickel
   15 pennies + 2 nickels
   10 pennies + 3 nickels
   5 pennies + 4 nickels
   5 nickels
   1 dime + 15 pennies
   1 dime + 10 pennies + 1 nickel
   1 dime + 5 pennies+ 2 nickels
   1 dime + 3 nickels
   2 dimes + 5 pennies
   2 dimes + 1 nickel